Caught

in

the

Middle

Caught

in

the

Middle

Alys Swan-Jackson

Piccadilly Press • London

For my Mother

Text copyright © Alys Swan-Jackson, 1997

Phototypeset from author's disk by Piccadilly Press.
Printed and bound in Hungary by Interpress,
for the publishers Piccadilly Press Ltd.,
5 Castle Road, London NW1 8PR.

Designed by Paul Cooper Design

A catalogue record for this book is available from the British Library

ISBN: 1 85340 389 X (trade paperback)
1 85340 384 9 (hardback)

Alys Swan-Jackson is British and lives in Hampstead, London. She is a freelance journalist and author of a number of children's non-fiction books. This is her first book for Piccadilly Press.

Acknowledgements

Thanks to Hampstead School, Parliament Hill School and the individuals who kindly completed the questionnaire, and to the following individuals and organisations which supplied reference material and advice:
The Brook Advisory Centre, The Philippa Fawcett Library, Simone E Katzenberg (Solomon, Taylor & Shaw, Solicitors), Relate and The Trust for the Study of Adolescence

Contents

*intro*duction

intro duction

"Everyone thinks their parents will stay together forever. When you find out that they're splitting up it can really knock you for six."
Mark (15)

Every year, around 200,000 children and young people learn that their parents are going to split up. Sometimes the split is temporary, but usually it's permanent.

In addition, more than 50% of those parents will re-marry within five years, and their children will find themselves members of step-families.

From what teenagers say, it's clear that when it comes to divorce or separation, they have enormously varied experiences. In some cases, violence is involved, or one parent disappears off the scene completely. In others, the separation seems quite amicable and is carefully planned so that children can have access to both parents.

Whatever happens, divorce or separation is a major alteration in family circumstances. Most teenagers will experience some pain and unhappiness. However, there may be benefits too, like the opportunity to take on new responsibilities and learn new skills.

Dealing with a break-up is never easy. You have to remember that it is not a single event, but an ongoing process of re-adjustment for everyone involved. As you can see from the experiences of the young people who have contributed to this book, you can go through many difficult times before you and your parents are able to come through and adjust to your new lives.

This is inevitable, but there are things that you can do to help yourself. Take encouragement from all the other people in this book who have survived and are able to be positive about what has happened.

Life goes on!

ALYS SWAN -JACKSON
1997

*B*reaking Up Is Hard To Do

Finding Out

Did you have any idea your parents were splitting up? How did they break the news?

I asked

"Because my mum owned a shop, and we lived out in the countryside, Mum and Dad were often having rows about what Mum would do if she got snowed in at her shop which was in a town nearby. One day they said they were arguing about it but it was in the summer, so I thought it was a bit strange. Then, when my mum came to kiss me goodnight that evening, I asked her if that was really what they were arguing about and she said no, and that she and Dad had been discussing a trial separation. I was very upset, hurt and confused."
   Carla (14)

They told me

"I wasn't surprised they split, because they'd been arguing a lot and not really speaking to each other.

After they told me, the tension at home got higher, because my dad didn't want to move out and my mum was really unhappy because she wanted him to go and they were arguing about that as well. It was a bit like a war zone at home."

Peter (13)

"I was going to a movie with my friend Jane, when Dad said he had something to tell me. He said he was going to move out. He and Mum thought it would be better if they lived apart."

Louise (16)

Mum just left home

"I'll always remember the day Mum left. Dad took me and my brother to Thorpe Park, and when we got home there was a note on the kitchen table from Mum saying she had left home."

Ann (17)

I overheard a conversation

"When I went to bed, I could hear my mum and dad talking. I heard my name a lot, and I know I shouldn't have done but I listened outside the door and I realised they were talking about divorce. Soon after, my mum told me she and Dad were splitting up. I didn't let on I knew anything, but it really hit me then, that Dad was going, and might not come back."

Miriam (17)

"I wasn't that surprised, because I'd heard them talk about separating before, but I was quite surprised because they hadn't been arguing that much recently. My dad told me that he was out looking at a flat to live in, but he said it was only temporary. They had intended for my mum to tell me, but it hadn't worked out. I felt really upset and quite shocked."
Louise (16)

Although it seemed to Louise like the end of the world, it wasn't. The same will be true for you.

For most parents, you – the teenager – will be almost the first consideration when they discuss splitting up. They will do the best they can for you. You might start to think they're obsessed by their own problems and haven't thought about what you're feeling. This is tough – as a teenager you've got enough to deal with. However, as this book will demonstrate, many teenagers have been there before and survived.

Have You Been Kept In The Dark?

"It was obvious that something serious was happening. Things had begun to go rapidly downhill between my parents. However, nobody told us. We felt like we didn't exist."
Olivia (15)

You naturally want to be told what's going on right at the beginning, and to find out what's going to happen to you. However, most parents find it difficult to

explain to their children why they are splitting up.
There are many reasons for this.

- If it's obvious to them why they are splitting up, and what's going to happen to the family, they mistakenly assume it's obvious to you too.

- They might feel they are protecting you by not discussing the break-up. Parents often don't realise that teenagers have a lot more understanding than they're given credit for, and are mature enough to make their own judgement.

- They may not be aware how much you need to know what's going on.

- They are probably having such a hard time themselves they have not stopped to think about what you feel. It could be that your parents are under so much stress that they can't focus on you.

- Some parents feel guilty because they think they've let you down.

- They may have been hoping to patch things up, and only decided to say something to you when it was obvious that there wasn't a chance of sorting things out.

- There might be so much hostility that they can't even talk to each other to discuss what's going to happen.

The best thing you can do to get as much information as possible is to ask your parents what is going to happen. Unfortunately, some parents don't even think to ask their children for their opinions, so it's important to tell your parents what you want. Make sure you pick a convenient time – not, for example, when your mum or dad have come home exhausted from a hard day at work. If you don't know how to begin, say something like, "Mum (Dad) – there are a few things that have been bothering me. Can we talk?" Explain that, even if they can't tell you immediately, they need to keep you informed so that you will feel less confused and afraid. If this is difficult, try writing them a note explaining how you feel and what you need to know. Make certain that you include some loving words in it as they are needing as much reassurance as you are at this time.

"It took a while for me to understand that Mum and Dad were so upset about the split themselves that they forgot that we were hurting too, and needed their support."
Carla (14)

How Long Will It Take?

The whole process of splitting up will probably take much longer than you'd like – a month, three months, even a year. It's very common for couples to make several attempts at reconciliation. One of your parents may move in and out of the house several times before they decide to make the final break. This is exceptionally tough on you, because you get your hopes up that they'll get back together and then they are dashed again. It's probably best to assume that once your parents have told you they're going to split up they probably will.

Immediate Reactions

"I was 13 when Dad broke the news to me. I can't say I was surprised. They were always arguing, so I was relieved, really. At first I felt sad that they couldn't be together, but I thought that from now on things can only get better. At least they won't be at each other's throats all the time."
Louise (16)

"I was gutted. I thought, this isn't supposed to happen. I screamed at them, 'I hate you, why are you doing this to me?'"
Paula (15)

"I was stunned. Mum just walked out one day. She left a note on the kitchen table saying she wasn't coming back. I know Mum and Dad argued a lot, but lots of parents do. I never dreamt she'd go like she did. I couldn't work it out."
Michael (18)

As you can see from these teenagers, initial reactions to the news can be varied. However much you might have expected a split, it's always upsetting when you're actually told. Most people take their parents' being together for granted, and something you've always taken for granted has come to an end.

There are common feelings experienced which are discussed in more detail in Chapter 5. Finding out that others felt the same way as you do now is often not only reassuring, but can fill you with a real sense of relief.

The Top Ten Questions Teenagers Ask Their Parents When They First Find Out

1. What happened that caused you to split up?
2. Will your separation be temporary or permanent?
3. Are you going to get divorced?
4. Are either of you going to marry someone else?
5. Where am I going to live?
6. Which of you will I be living with?
7. What are the arrangements for me to see the parent I'm not living with?
8. Will I still be able to see the rest of the family – grandparents, uncles, aunts etc?
9. Will I have to change schools?
10. What shall I tell people who ask what's going on?

You can write your questions down, so that you are prepared. You might even consider keeping a diary to record your feelings and help you determine what you want.

Talking and listening are the key to communication. This isn't easy when everyone seems to be on opposite sides or is on the offensive. Asking questions helps you deal with your feelings of fear and uncertainty. These feelings aren't going to disappear unless they are faced head-on. Not only will you feel better yourself, but your parents (and other people) can help you more if they know how you feel; the average parent isn't a mind-reader. By listening, you can see your parents' problems from their perspective which will help you to understand everything. Try and keep a calm head and an open mind.

Remember that your parents might not answer any of these questions. Be patient – they will probably answer them eventually.

two
*B*efore the Split

"I think the worst thing was how much they hated each other and how mean they were to each other all the time. They were always arguing and carrying on, big rows that would end with one of them storming out banging the door behind them. I really hated it, and I couldn't do anything about it."
Michael (18)

Conflict between parents is very hard for teenagers to deal with. It is the most upsetting aspect of life before, after and during a divorce or separation, and probably has the most far reaching effects.

Was Life Before The Split Really So Great?

It's easy to blame everything on your parents splitting up and think that if they hadn't separated, you'd be happy.

Be honest. Do you remember life before the split as a bed of roses? The chances are it wasn't that great. Nobody is happy all the time, and everyone has to face family problems of one sort or another – minor ones like being embarrassed by your parents, or major ones such as divorce and separation. As your parents were unhappy, life before the split was probably very tough. The chances are they behaved in one of these ways:

The Top Ten Ways Parents Handle Problems

1   Fight hammer and tongs.

2   Leave the room.

3   Don't say anything.

4   Always give in to the other's demands in order to keep the peace.

5   Scream and cry.

6   Get depressed.

7   Use drink, drugs or over-indulge in food.

8   Try to blame the problem on the other parent.

9   Get involved with someone else.

10 Resort to physical violence. Did your dad hit your mum or vice versa?

The break-up of a marriage is such a very tense time as these teenagers remember:

They were always arguing

"My parents were always arguing. Mum slagged off Dad, Dad went down the pub slamming the door. It seemed sort of normal. Then one day Mum and Dad sat us down and asked us how we'd feel if they split up. I was gob-smacked."
James (15)

"My mum and dad were always fighting. It was a real shock when they decided to divorce, but it was a relief too."
Jane (15)

If your parents have always had rows then you might not have realised that anything more serious than usual was going on.

Rows can occur in the best regulated families; indeed some families seem to thrive on them. Rows help clear the air. They can be the first step to problem solving.

However, if the rows are very frequent, or very unpleasant, it becomes something else. Sometimes parents can be getting on so badly that they use any excuse for an argument:

"My parents always argued a bit, but then they really started going over the top. They were really getting on each other's nerves. I think it was when they had a massive row about mum leaving some potato peelings in the sink that I realised there wasn't much hope for their marriage!"
Jade (18)

My dad used to beat up mum

Physical abuse is very serious. Did your dad beat your mum up? Perhaps it happened the other way round. It's very scary.

"My dad used to beat Mum up when he was drunk. I didn't know what to do. I wanted to help her, but I just buried my head under the bedclothes and pretended nothing was happening."
Donna (14)

The breakdown of the family relationship can take a long time – months or even years! Jane's parents' relationship had been teetering on the edge for the last year. Both of them were holding down high pressured, high powered jobs. They barely had time for each other. They didn't talk for days on end, and when they did, it ended up as a slanging match, each one hurling abuse at the other.

Eventually things came to a head.

"Mum discovered Dad was having an affair. She overheard him talking on the phone to his girlfriend and that was it really. They had a big fight, really physical. Mum beat Dad up pretty badly. She kept hitting him with a wine bottle. I couldn't bear it. I wanted them to stop, but I didn't know how to stop them. That fight was the first time the subject of divorce came up.

"Mum and Dad could see I was upset. They said whatever happened they'd see I was OK and that they would go and see a counsellor person who would help them decide what to do."
Jane (15)

They hardly talked to each other

In many ways, the worst kind of "not getting along" is when parents just don't communicate with each other at all. They avoid each other's company and don't speak to each other. Sometimes one of them always goes along with what the other one wants, just for the sake of avoiding any confrontation. Silent parents can mean there's an unbearably tense atmosphere at home.

"My parents are getting divorced. They hardly do anything together, and if they talk to each other at all they have a big fight."
   Darren (16)

"My dad's always in the pub. He's hooked on booze. I hate it when he comes home with a bad smell on his breath. If I have a go at him, he just says it helps him cope with stress."
   Donna (14)

I thought they got on really well

Usually, if you think back to how your parents were getting on before the split, you'll remember that there were signs that things weren't going well, even if you didn't notice them at the time.

However, sometimes things seem really normal and your parents appear to be getting along fine. This can make the split particularly difficult.

"My parents are splitting up. It's a real shock. I thought they got on really well. They never had rows. Mum always did what Dad wanted. I don't understand why they're splitting up."
   Chris (15)

Sometimes parents seem fine in public, even if they're obviously not getting on so well at home.

"I'd lie in bed listening to them shouting, but I didn't think it was that bad. They never argued in front of me or Gran or anyone. They carried on like normal, although it was obvious it was a bit of a strain. It never occurred to me they'd break up."
   Paula (15)

This can be really tough because it's so confusing and you might think you're imagining problems.

Keeping The Relationship Together

Is it possible that your parents could still stay together?

It's very easy to think that if your parents approached the problem in the right way, a split could be prevented.

There are ways of dealing with marital problems, if the couple fail to resolve them by themselves. It can be valuable to seek the assistance of a third party. This could be a family member or a mutual friend.

There are also various organisations of which Relate is probably the best known, which can give help and advice.

A counsellor got them talking

Problems don't disappear unless they are forced out into the open. The only option is to talk about them, however unpleasant and depressing it might be. It's often helpful to talk to someone who's completely objective, and this is where a counsellor comes in.

The counsellor won't necessarily help your parents stay together. If it's clear to them that there's no way of saving the relationship, or if either of your parents is absolutely set on separation, then the counsellor will assist them in making the split as easy as possible given the circumstances.

> *"My parents went to see a Relate counsellor who got them talking to each other again. It didn't stop the divorce going ahead, but at least it was less nasty than it might have been."*
> **John (16)**

Trial separations

Separation and divorce are quite different. If your parents separate, they will usually live apart, although they might, generally for financial reasons, continue living in the same house but sleep in separate bedrooms, and eat meals or go out socially separately.

Separation has no legal implications. If your parents decide to get back together, the absent parent can simply return. This is difficult for you, because you feel that your parents are neither married nor divorced, and you are uncertain what is going to happen next.

Some separations are temporary. They give your parents time to think things over and decide what they want to do. It is a good time for them to go to a counsellor or group counselling. If your parents have just split up, and they haven't sought the help of a counsellor before, it might be worth suggesting it to them.

If one of your parents visits a solicitor, don't immediately jump to the conclusion that a divorce is underway. Some people visit a solicitor to get information. If it worries you, talk to trusted friends and relatives or ask your parents what's happening – even if what they have to say isn't good. Don't pretend everything is OK when it isn't.

If your parents do have a trial separation, you should realise that they're unlikely to get back together. Because you (and any brothers and sisters you might have) are involved, most parents will have tried *everything* first and only decided to separate as a last resort.

Once your parents have thought it through they will reach a decision. If they decide to divorce or separate permanently then you have to accept that there's nothing you can do.

three
*I*f only I'd...

Even though, deep down, you probably know you're not responsible for your parents splitting up, it's really common for teenagers to feel that, somehow, they might have contributed to the break-up.

"The worst thing was the hate between them. They really hated each other. All they'd do was slag each other off to me all the time. I hated being caught in the middle of it. I couldn't stop them. I tried to tell myself it's not my fault, but I couldn't. I should have been able to stop them."
Rachel (16)

Why Teenagers Feel Responsible

Life is very complicated when your parents are breaking up. On the one hand you are probably feeling relieved that a long period of rows and tension is over, but on the other hand you're hoping that your parents will work it out and get back together. Even if they were rowing, at least they were both still around. Then you have to face up to the fact that the separation or divorce is going to go ahead.

Why has this happened? Was it my fault? Was it something I did? are typical reactions.

If only I'd done what they wanted

"My first thought was, this is all my fault. I remembered all the times I'd argued with Mum and Dad and carried on if I didn't get my own way. If only I'd done what they wanted, this would never have happened."
   Darren (16)

"My parents separated when I was 16. It seems ridiculous now, but when Mum left, my first thought was I should have done better in my GCSEs. She was really upset when I got bad grades, and I said to myself, if I'd worked a little bit harder, done a little bit better she'd never have got upset and left us like she did."
   Michael (18)

Mum blamed me

Sometimes, in a fit of pique, one of your parents might have blamed you, and said something like, "No wonder Dad didn't want to hang around when you're so moody all the time," – or whatever. At this emotional time, it's sadly not surprising when parents (or anyone else involved) say the first thing which comes into their head and which they don't mean.

They argued about me

"I was quite a rebel and my parents were always arguing about how to deal with me. When they told me they were getting a divorce I just knew it was because of me, and I felt terrible. Then I talked to Gran, and she told me that they'd just have found something else to argue about if I hadn't been there."
   Jade (18)

I kept asking for things

"I felt really guilty. I knew they were having money problems. I thought, it's all my fault because I keep asking them for new trainers and stuff."
Peter (13)

As a teenager you're more likely to feel responsible than if you're younger. For one thing, teenagers often have a volatile relationship with their parents. You want to go out with your friends, you want to buy clothes, you want to stay out late. But however much you have infuriated your parents recently, you certainly aren't to blame for the failure of their relationship.

You realise that you're responsible for yourself, and you can start feeling responsible for other people. But you're not – they, and they alone are responsible for their actions.

Why It's Not Your Fault

The only people who are responsible for the split are your parents.

Because your parents are adults and their relationship is separate from yours, however difficult you might have been, you can't influence it. Remember that the split is between your parents, not you and your parents. Your parents' love for you is unconditional; their love for each other is not. Unfortunately most parents will be so stressed out that they cannot show that they love you. Try hard, if you can, to let them them know that you love them.

Strategies To Help You Realise It's Not Your Fault

- Write down the reasons *you* think your parents are splitting up.

- Pick out all the things you think *you* did to cause the split. Write them down too.

- Look at your lists. Think of what you might have done differently. Would that have helped?

- Ask yourself honestly if you are involved. When you think about it, you must realise nothing you did could have affected your parents' relationship. Would you really have had that much influence over your parents. It's more likely you share Donna's experience.

"My parents never let me do what I wanted, so I had a real go at them. My mate though, she was good as gold. It didn't do either of us any good. She never got her way either. And both our parents ended up divorced."
Donna (14)

If you still believe you're responsible, you should talk to someone who can give you an objective opinion. You'll certainly find they tell you it's not your fault.

Some of the reasons for your parents' divorce are explained in the next chapter.

four

Why Relationships Fail

"I asked my dad if he loved my mum and he didn't answer."
   Chris (15)

"Mum told me Dad had left and wasn't coming back. He'd run off with another woman."
   Carla (14)

So who's to blame? Maybe some fault lies with both parents.

When they first get married, or move in with each other a couple usually has the best of intentions. Very few people make commitments without truly believing and wanting it to last forever.

Even Your Parents Were Young And In Love Once

You know the reasons why couples decide to live together in the first place:

- Sexual attraction.

- They are in love.

- They get on very well.

- The woman is pregnant.
- They are scared of being alone.
- It is cheaper to have one home instead of two.

You can probably think of loads of other reasons, but as you can see, none of the reasons are necessarily permanent – couples can fall out of love, sexual attraction can pall, once they really get to know each other they discover they are actually very different people...

The Top Ten Reasons Why Couples Split Up

1 One or both parents are no longer in love with the other.

2 Lack of money (often caused by unemployment).

3 Partners feel that they cannot lead a happy, fulfilled life with each other any more.

4 One or both parents have met someone else.

5 Both partners realise they are not compatible.

6 Both partners have different expectations.

7 Domestic violence, and other unreasonable behaviour.

8 Divorces are easier to obtain.

9 There is no longer any stigma attached to divorce.

10 Expectations aren't met.

It's worth looking at some of these reasons a bit closer.

They drifted apart

"My mum and dad both worked really hard and they both liked doing different things when they had any free time. They told me they'd just drifted apart without really realising it and didn't have much in common any more."
Sarah (16)

When relationships do break down, the couple involved often don't realise anything is seriously wrong until it's too late. Maybe they've refused to acknowledge the problems.

They've started to lead separate lives and one day one or both of them just realise they shouldn't be together any more.

They couldn't cope with dad's redundancy

"My dad got made redundant a year ago. He hasn't found another job and he just hangs around the house all day watching TV. My mum hates it. She's always on at him, and bitching about how we can't have things because there isn't any money."
Warren (15)

Parents have to have a strong relationship in order to cope with difficult times – like money shortages or a severe illness. In such situations marriages often either collapse or get stronger. And if a couple is already having problems, pressures of any kind can be the final blow.

Mum and dad never saw each other

Many couples find themselves working long hours in order to achieve a good standard of living, often at the expense of their families. Karen's father had a job that entailed a lot of travelling. He was hardly ever at home. Karen's mother went along with this, but kept hoping that her husband would work in something less demanding. One day he told them that he had taken a job in another city, and that the whole family had to move. That was too much for Karen's mum, who decided she wanted to separate.

Dad had an affair

Often one of your parents will have had an affair, or met someone else. If your mum (or dad) has an affair, it doesn't necessarily mean she (he) wants to break up. However, if the other parent finds out about the affair they might feel so betrayed that they want the marriage to end. Alternatively, your mum or dad might think they can lead a happier life with the other person.

"Mum found out Dad was having an affair and now he's moved out. He doesn't love us any more."
Rachel (16)

"Dad took us out to dinner and said he was sorry, but he felt he had to leave. He was in love with someone else, and couldn't live without her."
John (16)

Dad's an alcoholic

Sometimes unjustifiable behaviour is to blame. Violence, which is often fuelled by alcohol or drugs,

---
34
---

from one partner to the other, or even to the children can cause a breakdown in the relationship.

"My dad's an alcoholic. Mum put up with Dad's drinking for years. Then one night he got so drunk he nearly killed her and she threw him out."
Stephen (16)

Although it may seem obvious to the outside world that the best thing to do is to get out of an abusive relationship, the people involved often find it a very difficult and frightening thing to deal with. Most often the abused parent thinks that they can help. It can take a long time to accept that often they can't.

"Dad always liked a drink, but then he started drinking really heavily. He'd get drunk and pass out somewhere, and me and my mum would have to fetch him and bring him home. I think that's the reason my parents split up."
Tina (15)

Adults – Tina's dad for example – often use alcohol, drugs, or food to help them cope with stress. If you see that your parents are hooked, you will have to accept that there is nothing *you* can do to make them kick the habit. No amount of begging, crying or protesting is going to work. However, don't ignore it. Never cover up for them or make excuses for their behaviour. Deal with your own feelings instead. If you are feeling angry or ashamed, you can seek the help and advice of organisations such as Alateen, which was established specifically to support the children of problem drinkers. You can find a list of some of them in Chapter 12.

Many counsellors advocate "tough" love which means not supporting and propping up the addict, and sometimes the partner who has a problem is cured after a divorce.

There's no stigma attached to divorce

In recent years, divorce has become much more common. Current statistics for the UK indicate that one in three marriages will fail. Even thirty years ago divorces were difficult to obtain and there was a tremendous stigma attached. Couples often put up with unhappy marriages rather than suffer the humiliation of getting divorced. Happily, attitudes towards breaking up have changed. These days people expect to live happy, successful, fulfilled lives, and sometimes they don't find it with their partner.

They both gave me different reasons

"What really upset me is that both my parents gave me totally different reasons for the divorce. I was very confused. I thought – which one of them is lying? If my parents could have given me good reasons why, instead of just bitching at each other, I would have felt far less hurt."
Donna (14)

Perhaps there genuinely are a lot of different reasons why your parents are splitting up. It might be difficult for both of them to put a finger on one specific problem. But if you are unhappy about anything you've been told, asking one or both your parents is the best thing to do.

They won't give me a reason

If your parents either refuse to talk to you, or don't give you an explanation that satisfies you, you will have to ask for one directly. Ask them why they are splitting up, and what's going to happen next. If they don't answer, talk to someone who might be able to help – a grandparent or a family friend for instance. Doing so, should reassure you, and make you feel less anxious and uncertain.

Don't Take Sides

It's very easy to take sides when your parents split up; it's extremely easy if you're closer to one parent than the other. It means you might get a very one-sided view of the split.

If one of your parents had an affair, is an alcoholic or has an extremely difficult personality for instance, you're likely to blame that parent for the split. But remember that only your parents know what really went on in their marriage. There are a lot of things which you may know nothing about. What is important for you to understand is that your parents still love you, even if they are no longer in love with each other. You don't have to cover up for them and you don't owe one parent more loyalty than the other. If you don't understand why one parent is cheating on the other or feel worried or afraid, ask them to explain. You'll feel better.

Most couples who have split up, finally separate on average a year or two after the subject first arises. By then, they are quite sure they will never get back together again. If they believe that the end of the partnership is for the best, you have, whatever your feelings, to accept the inevitable.

five

How Do You Feel?

It's impossible to describe all the different feelings you can experience days, weeks, months, even years after you learn that your parents are going to split up. Shock, anger, sadness, fear, denial and depression are just a few of the powerful feelings that teenagers have said they experienced. The strength of these feelings will depend on a lot of things, particularly how your parents broke the news to you, how much conflict there is at home, and what sort of custody and access arrangements are agreed.

Shock

"At first I was in shock. I couldn't talk, I couldn't think. I just felt totally dazed."
  Jessica (15)

Shock is often the initial reaction to a traumatic experience and it can take many different forms.

Jane wandered around in a complete daze and became absent-minded, careless and clumsy. You may feel like crying or just yelling out loud and you may not want to speak to anyone. Jane says,

"I went to my room and put my music on really loud so that no one would hear me, and screamed and screamed."
  Jane (15)

Other teenagers had similar experiences.

"I was gutted. I started screaming and swearing and crying."
   Donna (14)

"I was completely stunned...I couldn't believe that Mum would leave like she did and she wasn't coming back."
   Lizzie (18)

"At first, I didn't have any reaction at all. I felt numb. I suppose I was in shock."
   Michael (18)

"I remember feeling totally cut off from normal life. I spent most of the time lying in bed, crying."
   Natasha (15)

Shock is a perfectly normal, understandable response. These kinds of impulses are your body's natural defence system coming into play – to protect you through this difficult time. However, feelings of shock shouldn't be ignored. Go and see your doctor if the physical symptoms are too hard to bear: if you feel constantly tired and depressed, or you can't eat. It may be a good opportunity to talk about what's happened, and how you feel about it.

Anger

"When they told me, I felt angry and very unhappy."
   Paula (15)

It's very common to feel an explosive anger after the initial shock passes. Many teenagers feel that their parents have let them down and messed up their lives because they've split up. You'll probably be thinking, "How dare they do this!" or, "What about me?" It will all seem very unfair and you may well want to punch or kick something.

Anger can be a particularly difficult emotion to deal with. You're unable to express it to the parent who isn't around any more, and you might think that showing it will only make the situation worse. As a result, a lot of anger can be swallowed up and never let out.

You need to find an outlet for your anger, but there are good ways and bad ways:

"I felt terrible, I just couldn't cope, and I really rebelled. I played truant from school, went out with my mates and got drunk, did a few drugs. Mum went mad and yelled a lot, but I didn't take any notice."
Darren (16)

Darren's mum felt unable to do anything. She had a lot of problems maintaining discipline, she felt very guilty about what had happened and consequently let Darren do pretty much as he liked. Darren for his part, wanted to push his mum as far as he could, just to see how much he could get away with. Although this sort of rebellion is extreme behaviour, Darren was actually wanting his mother's attention and her love.

"I got arrested for being drunk and disorderly and had to go to court. Luckily, I was let off with a caution because it was my first offence, but I won't do that again."
Darren (16)

Tess felt as if she didn't have a home to go to any more:

"My parents divorced when I was thirteen. By the time I was sixteen, I was going out practically every night, and when I met Dave I decided to live with him. I left school and found a job as a secretary."
Tess (20)

In retrospect, Tess feels some regret.

"I was far too young, but I felt that I knew best. At 16, I wanted my own life. I do regret leaving school. I probably would have got a better job if I'd stuck it out, but nobody said anything. My parents seemed so caught up with their own lives, they didn't seem interested. Dave and I are getting married, there doesn't seem anything else to do."
Tess (20)

Using drugs or alcohol to numb the pain is not a good idea. They cannot provide any permanent solution to your problems, they'll just give you a few more to deal with. All they do is temporarily cover up your feelings. When you're sober those feelings will still be there.

Some teenagers take their anger out on the people closest to them – their friends or the parent they live with. Although they might understand, it's not really very fair to them and it'll probably make you feel guilty.

A more positive way of dealing with anger is to do some kind of physical exercise, such as going for a run or playing sport. Physical exertion makes you forget yourself, and makes you feel more optimistic in your outlook. It can help stop you from lying awake and thinking gloomy thoughts every night. You'll wake up feeling more refreshed and better able to cope. Fitness brings other benefits too. It makes you look trim and helps add to your attraction – which, for teenagers, is particularly important! Drugs and alcohol abuse do the opposite: they interfere with healthy sleep patterns and make you slobby, spotty and unattractive. All of this does nothing for your confidence and self esteem!

Pain

"I just cried and cried. I remembered all the good times we'd had and how much things had changed."
Jane (15)

Strong pain and an acute feeling of loss often take the place of anger. These feelings will probably last for a long time, making you feel sad and depressed. The onset of grief is very natural, as you begin to mourn the loss of your old life. It's not necessary to "put on a brave face".

Crying really does help. If you can cry outwardly, you can begin to release all those pent-up emotions you are holding inside. And once you can do that, you can begin to deal with things.

Loss

"I got really upset about the whole situation. Dad was horrible to Mum, and I took Mum's side even though I didn't want to take sides. I thought if Dad moves out it can only get better. But it hasn't worked out that way, I know what my dad's like, but I wish he was still here."
Jason (16)

Separation and divorce are often compared to death. Even though the parent who moves out hasn't actually died, some of the feelings you will experience are very similar. Loss is one of these. The loss of a parent through divorce or separation can be even more difficult to bear. At least after a death people generally remember the dead person with affection, and there is none of the bitterness and recrimination which are the hallmark of many split-ups. Death also has a finality about it – you won't see the dead person again. If your parent has moved out – particularly if they just walked out or have moved a long way away – you have all the uncertainty of not really knowing if, and when, you will see them again.

Another important thing to realise is that loss in this case doesn't just mean loss of the absent parent. If you move house and change schools you can lose your friends; you can lose a whole set of relations – grandparents, cousins etc. You might even feel that you have lost the affection of the parent you live with, particularly if they start to work long hours and have less time to spend with you, and the strain of the divorce and lone-parenting makes them tired and irritable.

These losses combine to make you feel like you have lost the normal things in life that others take for granted. But you *can* do your best to prevent losing contact with people – see Chapter 7 for details.

Rejection

"I remember my one concern being that if my mum didn't live with us she didn't love me any more. As long as she loved me I didn't worry what was happening."
Lizzie (18)

Rejection is another common feeling. While you might know, deep down, that the lost parent hasn't deliberately turned their back on you, it still feels like it. This is especially true if a parent has walked out, particularly if it's to live with another partner and even more so if that partner has children. However much explanation you get, whatever reasons you've been given, you still can't help feeling that your parent has double-crossed you.

"Dad went to live with Sarah and her two children. I wasn't getting on that well with Mum and I wanted to go and live with him, but he said it would be really difficult. He'd rejected Mum and then I really felt he was rejecting me."
Jade (18)

Fear

"I felt scared. I thought, 'What's going to happen....? Where am I going to live...? Can I still see my dad?'"
Jessica (15)

Change can be a major source of stress, primarily because it's easy to be overcome with fear of the unknown. You probably feel scared and vulnerable. Of course you know there are going to be changes, but perhaps no one has talked to you about them or asked your opinion. This kind of uncertainty can be very worrying. Jane and her younger sister, Anita, live in the country miles away from their school and have to travel there by car.

"We talked about it all the time. If Dad's not here any more, who's going to drive us to school in the morning?"
Jane (15)

There'll be so many questions that will arise when this sort of thing happens, and as a teenager you might find yourself having to ask them all. Many parents will not have thought about the logistics.

Denial

"I thought, if I wait long enough, Mum and Dad will get back together and it will be like it was before. That's what I wanted."
Paula (15)

It's very common to deny to yourself that your parents' separation is really happening. Many teenagers try to persuade themselves that the situation is only temporary, and sooner or later, their parents will get back together. This is particularly true if parents have a second go at their relationship, before they finally break up, or if your parents made a real effort to have a smooth split, and still get on well together.

"I tried really hard. When we went out on my birthday I kept pointing out to Dad how great Mum looked. Like, she'd lost all this weight and wore this really nice dress, not her old jeans like she usually does. I said, go on dad, give her a kiss, but he wouldn't. He looked really embarrassed."
Paula (15)

The "happy ending" as Paula subsequently discovered, rarely happens in practice. Divorce or separation isn't usually a spur of the moment thing, and your parents have probably reached that decision after a lot of thought and painful consideration. Hard as it is, it's more realistic to accept the break-up as permanent and begin to get used to it. Once you have accepted the inevitable, you'll start to feel better. Much later on, you'll recognise you've come through it, and most important of all, you can get on with your own life.

Relief

Sometimes it comes as a relief, particularly if one of your parents has behaved in a violent or intolerable way.

"My mum and dad were always fighting. It was my dad mostly. To be honest, I just wanted him to go away and leave us alone. I hated him."
  Stephen (16)

Conflict and continuous disagreement create tension. Neither of your parents will have a lot of time for helping you in the ways that you think you need. A partnership has to work. The reality is that there is not a great deal that you can do about it. You may not be aware of all the issues at first. Perhaps a separation is best for everyone.

Ten Great Ways To Cope If You've Hit Rock-bottom

1   Eat ice-cream.

2   Go shopping.

3   Soak in the bath for half an hour.

4   Listen to some music.

5   Have a big night out with your mates.

6   Go for a work-out.

7   Get your mates to come round and slag off your parents for a few hours.

8   Spend a day in the country.

9   Scream and shout.

10   Think positive. Things can only get better.

six

*I*mmediate practical changes

A Parent Moving Out

As soon as your parents have made the decision to split up, or at least separate for a while, one of them will almost certainly move out, and establish a "second home".

"My mum moved out, and I think I miss having her around more than my brother. Dad doesn't talk about clothes or boyfriends or other girl stuff. It makes me wish my mum was around more."
Kate (12)

It's hard to actually *believe* a split is happening until a parent moves out so it will inevitably make you feel sad. Give yourself time and space to think about how you can maintain contact with the parent who has left. Can you talk on the telephone every day? What sort of visits can you arrange? Don't believe you are making a favourite of one parent, or being disloyal to the other. Continued contact with the absent parent will, in most cases, make you feel happier, and more confident. See Chapter 7 for more information.

You Moving

You may find that you have to make major changes yourself, such as moving into a new house or starting at a new school.

"I decided who I wanted to live with. I only moved 6 miles away from my dad and I had to change schools anyway, so I went to the same one I would have gone to if they hadn't split up. But it was difficult living in a different house as it was a lot smaller."
   Louise (16)

"I was very upset and incredibly excited. I knew we had moved from Birmingham to London because my dad's family were there and he needed them for support."
   Michael (18)

You have to allow for a period of adjustment. Finding your way around, and making new friends takes time. It can even be a welcome distraction:

"I had so much new stuff to deal with that I couldn't just dwell on my mum and dad's divorce – I had to move on."
   Jade (18)

Having Less Money

"Dad said money was tight, and he had to reduce my spending money. I was really angry. I knew it was wrong, but when I saw his wallet lying around I helped myself."
   Freddie (16)

Money worries often magnify at this time, which can increase the stress at home. It's always more expensive to run two homes rather than one. Often the financial responsibilities will fall primarily on one parent. Maybe the absent parent isn't great at keeping up maintenance payments. There will frequently be less money available and if there's a choice between the gas bill and new clothes and entertainment you can guess which wins! Your parent may have to find a job or work longer hours. As a result you find yourself having to help out more at home.

"Before the divorce Mum didn't work and she'd put dinner on the table for us. Now she's working, she's always tired. She just comes in from work and collapses in front of the TV. I cook dinner and tidy up."
     Peter (13)

Nevertheless you shouldn't have to keep the household going. If you feel your parent is being unreasonable let him/her know this. You and your parent will feel better if you are both quite clear what is expected. Is it really serious if your bedroom is a mess? Isn't it better to cook dinner?

"I don't think Mum earns very much, so I work in a shop at weekends so that I can afford to buy clothes and go out."
     Rachel (16)

Lack of money can be particularly hard on you if, for example, your friends have more new clothes than you, but it's not the end of the world. Try to find ways of cutting down on spending. You can always earn some money yourself, like Rachel. If you're under sixteen, jobs like babysitting or newspaper rounds are available.

Money can also be the cause of arguments between your parents. Don't allow yourself to be involved.

seven

Relationships with your parents

"When Dad left, Mum used to cry all the time. She changed. I couldn't talk to her, she just didn't seem interested, so I just used to shut myself in my room and play my music really loud."
   Carla (14)

Understanding What They're Going Through

You can probably understand what your parents are going through to some extent. It's like splitting up with your boyfriend/girlfriend, but a million times worse. Most couples marry or live together thinking that it's going to be forever so when the unbelievable happens they are devastated.

How difficult the split is depends a lot on the circumstances. If one parent has just walked out with no prior warning, or the split was particularly nasty, then it will be extremely hard. If your parents have taken a long time to reach their decision, and it's mutual, then they may have done everything they can to lessen the blow. However, when it becomes a reality, feelings like shock, sadness, fear and guilt surface.

Mum had no warning at all

"Dad walked in and casually announced that he'd met someone else and was leaving. Mum was in shock – he'd given her no warning at all. They'd been together since they were 16 – my age..."
Rachel (16)

Mum misses him

It is quite a difference having to cope on your own when you are used to having another person around, however badly you got on with them. It seems a frightening prospect.

"I wish Mum didn't keep watching the phone. She pretends she doesn't but I know the feeling. She wants him to ring and say he's coming back. He's married again, but she's still waiting..."
Jade (18)

Mum has no confidence

If your mum or dad has been left for someone else, they will feel very unconfident, hurt, lonely and rejected. The parent who left will probably feel extremely guilty. Jason's parents separated and his dad moved out. For the first few months his mum was really depressed and cried all the time.

"She was really nervous and underconfident. I'd try and talk to her but half the time it was obvious she wasn't listening. Either that, or she'd make a big fuss of me and buy me lots of stuff. It only made me feel worse. I felt sorry for Mum, but I had my own problems. I really missed my dad and I was coping

with other things. I started secondary school and it was really difficult. Eventually I talked to my grandma about it, and she talked to my mum. It was great because Mum listened to her and she realised she shouldn't feel bitter and twisted about how things worked out."
   Jason (16)

Jason's mum was so crushed by the situation, that she didn't have enough energy to see to Jason's needs. Just when Jason most needed her help, she was unable to give him support. Fortunately Jason was able to talk to his grandma and things started to improve. His mother started to get used to her new life, and became far more relaxed.

Dad said he felt guilty

Parents will feel very guilty, not just about the end of the relationship and the mess they feel they are in, but because they are afraid of what it may have done to you.

"I thought Dad had what he wanted. Sarah's OK and she's quite pretty. Mum's great but she's let herself go. When Dad told me the other night how guilty he felt I was really surprised."
   Jade (18)

He's lost loads of friends

Splitting up with a partner means much more than losing that person. Friends of theirs may side with one or the other, especially old friends who will probably side with the one they knew first, even though they might have been close to the other parent. This is particularly true when it comes to relations – "blood is thicker than water".

It's also very hard because couples tend to know couples and socialise in couples. A single man or woman might suddenly find their social life has gone.

Mum went crazy

If you understand how bad your parents will be feeling, you'll be able to understand if, for instance, they start acting weirdly or become distant, irritable, or over-wrought. Sometimes the change is radical.

"My parents split up a year ago. Mum went crazy for a while. She lost a couple of stone, dyed her hair and did drink and drugs."
Paula (15)

At its most extreme it can appear that your parents don't love or care for you any more.

Supporting A Parent

"When my mum discovered Dad was having an affair, she was gob-smacked. She couldn't cope. She didn't go to work for a week, and was really miserable. I wanted to help, but I mean, what could I do? I had my own problems, to deal with. I wanted her to help me."
Jason (16)

"Mum couldn't cope. It wasn't like home because Mum was really upset most of the time. It was a bit tense. Mum was always careful not to slag Dad off in front of me, so I was able to continue living in my own naive

little world. Now, I think she felt rejected because Dad went off with someone else.

"I felt really angry with my dad. I think my dad's a bastard for what he did, not helping her through this bad time. The more I think about it the more I hate him because I feel he never liked me or cared. I don't think he realised he had kids. He was useless. He used to always keep himself to himself. "
Rachel (16)

It's a bit weird when your parents obviously need your help. You're probably used to your parents being there to help *you* and then the roles are reversed.

Mum always confided in me

Some parents will use their teenage children for emotional support. Jane's mum found it difficult to cope after her dad left and moved in with another woman.

"Mum leant on me. She's always confided in me and she told me how she felt. Sometimes I felt like I was the grown-up and she was the child."
Jane (15)

"I used to find Mum really embarrassing, but since the divorce we've got really close to each other. She's more like a sister than my mum."
Rachel (16)

Try to be sympathetic and understand how painful life is for them. Try not to give them a hard time or test them. It's often very difficult to think or act rationally when feelings are in turmoil. Stress can make people behave in very uncharacteristic ways. If, for example one parents slags the other off to you, even though they know they shouldn't, or talks obsessively about past history, realise that they are only giving way to feelings of hurt, anger and rejection. It's hard for your parent to come to terms with the loss of someone they once – perhaps still do – loved very much.

I did my bit

It's quite easy to help your mum or dad with the practical things. While you shouldn't have to run the whole household, you can do your bit:

"I offered to babysit my little sister once a week for free so Mum could go out and have a break."
Jade (18)

"My mum was in a really bad way, so I'd do the cooking and helped with the housework and a friend of my mum's helped out. It made me realise what a lot she'd done before."
Rachel (16)

Some people adapt to change more quickly than others. Eventually things will become easier, but it does require time and patience.

Caught In The Middle

Divorce is particularly hard if you're used as a weapon in the battle between parents, but if the divorce has been very nasty it's tempting for parents to do just that. They might slag each other off to you continually; they use you as a message-carrier; they force you to choose between your parents; one parent can be deliberately difficult about access, either by never being at the right place at the right time or finding reasons to change existing arrangements...

These are a few teenagers' experiences.

I felt like piggy in the middle

"I felt like piggy in the middle. My mum hated me talking about my dad. It was like he didn't exist, so I carried on talking about him and she thought I was just annoying her on purpose. I mean I love my dad. It really upset me."
Jane (15)

"My parents still fight about everything. They say really mean things to each other and then my mum cries. I can't stand it. I yell at them to stop but all they do is tell me to butt out. I don't know what to do."
Darren (16)

Darren felt sad and confused. His parents were behaving in ways that he didn't recognise. In this situation, it's very common for parents to forget the right way to behave.

They involved me in their fights

John was 13 when his parents divorced. Both of them decided that John ought to live with them and embarked on a long bitter fight for custody. There were constant rows:

"It was awful. Every time they had a fight they'd try and get me involved. Dad said he'd never agree to me living with Mum. Mum said he was a piss head and

said taking me down the club every night when he went drinking wasn't on. Dad said all she cared about was her new boyfriend. He made me say I wanted to live with him but when the social worker asked me where I wanted to go I just broke down and wouldn't say. I didn't know where I wanted to go, I just wanted someone to tell me where. I felt bad. Mum has this big family, but since my dad split up with his girlfriend he hasn't got anyone. He's just got me and I feel really sorry for him. Yeah, my dad drinks, he can be pretty awful but I can talk to him about things. Football. Mum isn't interested. It wasn't right. I was really fed up the way they played me off against each other."
John (16)

Dad asked me to spy on Mum

"Every time I see my dad he asks me what Mum's up to, if she's seeing anyone, stuff like that. Why doesn't he ask her instead of trying to get me to grass on her?"
Chris (15)

They got jealous over me

Donna's parents used her as a weapon.

"Sometimes, well, they'd both fight about me, or get jealous over me. They both said they wanted me to live with them, but I wanted to live with my gran. I kept telling them it was none of my business and to sort it themselves, but they didn't listen."
Donna (14)

Dealing With Conflict

Your parents have no right to try to make you take sides. The best thing to do is to tell them that you love them both, and you're not going to choose one of them over the other. If one parent asks you to spy on the other, tell them that if they want to know, they'll have to find out for themselves. Neither of your parents is owed more loyalty than the other. Never get involved in arguments. Simply walk away and leave them to get on with it. There's no point talking to them until they've stopped.

If the constant fights and slanging matches get you down, wait until things get calmer and tell them that you are fed up with all the arguments and bickering. That could be a real eye-opener! They may not even be aware of how you feel, and as a result they might be able to begin to understand what they are doing to themselves and to you.

If you find talking to them difficult, why not write them a letter? Writing things down can have other benefits too – it can help you organise your thoughts and feelings, and while it won't solve the problems, it may make you feel better.

Don't Apportion Blame

"I blame my mum. She's the one that had an affair in the first place. Then my dad went off and had an affair to get back at her."
Jessica (15)

Jessica felt very angry that her mum had an affair, and, as she saw it, was therefore responsible for the family breakdown. However, when both of them sat down and talked, and she got her mother's side of the story, Jessica's mum told her that she had felt very frustrated because her dad was a "workaholic" and worked late at the office every night, and at weekends.

It might seem obvious to you that one parent is to blame – for instance if, like Jessica, your mum had an affair first, your dad's an alcoholic, or one parent has walked out on the other.

Always remember there are things you don't know about and there are two sides to every situation.

Living With One Parent

Living with one parent instead of two is a big change. Usually, the parents decide who the children will live with, and sometimes they ask for their children's opinion. Deciding which parent to live with is a terrible decision to have to make, particularly if you just want to be with them both. Choosing who to live with is not choosing who you love most. The answer is to work out where you would feel happiest and most secure and to let your parents know.

Freddie, now 16, didn't want to live with his mum because he couldn't get along with her new partner.

"We were always arguing. She didn't like my mates coming over, and she was totally unreasonable about what time I came in of a night. I said I wanted to live with my dad – and I did."
   Freddie (16)

"It was obvious I was going to live with my mum because my dad's a singer and was often on tour and so I was used to having Mum around. Dad lives in the United States so I go for holidays and alternate Christmases."
Jessica (15)

In practice, it's still more common for children to stay with their mums, the argument being that mothers are more used to looking after them. This is untrue of course. Many fathers are just as good at parenting and many children live very happily with their dads.

All kinds of living arrangements are possible. Some children live with one parent most of the time, and see the other parent by arrangement. Some live first with one, and then the other on a short or long term basis. A few go through several changes. If parents can't reach a decision, then the Court together with you, will do it for them. (See Chapter 12)

The parent you see on a day to day basis is the one who sets the rules – telling you you have to be in by ten o'clock, making you do the household chores, getting you to do your homework. It's easy to think that if you were living with the other parent you would have a much better time; this is almost certainly untrue. Probably when you visit the parent you're not living with you do fun things – but remember, that's because you only see them occasionally and they can afford the time and money to treat you.

Keeping Up With The Absent Parent

A quarter of all teenagers with divorced parents lose contact with the absent parent after two years. The usual reasons are:

- Financial. Perhaps your parent lives in another country, and doesn't have the money to visit regularly.

- Inconvenience. If a parent lives far away it can be a lot of effort to visit. Perhaps there isn't any room for you to stay.

- Teenager doesn't want to see the parent. This usually happens if you blame the absent parent for the split.

Whoever you live with, you will inevitably miss the other parent, and they will miss you. Remember that just because one parent is not living with you, they are still your parent. It will probably not be so easy for them to show how much they care, particularly if they are living miles away, and only see you at half-term or holidays, but both of you can get over a lot of the difficulties by talking and taking the opportunity of showing care and concern. However hard it is, it's usually worth maintaining contact if you can, even by letter or telephone call, as you might regret it later on. Do persevere.

"Every weekend either my sister, myself or both of us stays Friday or Saturday night at my dad's house. He sometimes visits during the week. It's good because I still see my dad."
Louise (16)

It's up to me to make arrangements

"I see my dad once a week. It's up to me to make arrangements."
Paula (15)

"I lived with my mum for a while before I saw my dad properly. That really upset me, so I talked to Mum about it. Now I see Dad whenever I want to, mostly at weekends."
Jane (15)

He can't be bothered to see me

It can be very painful if you lose contact with one of your parents, if for example, he or she has moved out and has decided not to keep in touch.

"Since the split, I think Dad hates me, because he ignores me. He's not interested in anything I do, or what I've got to say. He couldn't even be bothered to come and see me in the school play."
Rachel (16)

Remember, things are not necessarily as they seem. For instance, if your dad's the "guilty party" – say he left your mum for another woman – he may feel very bad and think that you won't want to see him. Make sure your parents know that you want to keep in touch with both of them. Even if your parents are at loggerheads, you can make your own arrangements to see the other one. And don't feel as if you're betraying the parent you're living with – it's only natural to want to see both your parents, whatever happened.

It might be dangerous to see my dad

"My mum didn't want us to see my dad because he was dealing in drugs and she didn't want me to be caught up in the drugs. And I don't want to see him, I think he's a bastard for not helping my mum."
Rachel (16)

Very occasionally it might be dangerous for you to see one parent. Perhaps they're very violent or are drug addicts. Obviously you should listen to what people say, but if you really miss them, you might ask if this means *all* contact has to be broken – perhaps you could still phone or write to keep the contact going.

I don't want to see my dad

"My mum knew that I would never want to live with my dad. I don't want to see him, but my sister sees him."
Rachel (16)

Even if you don't want to see the absent parent now, you might change your mind in the future. Leave your options open – write or phone instead if you really don't want to see them.

I can talk to my dad now

There may be unexpected benefits in having two homes:

"Before the divorce, I didn't feel close to my dad. It was really difficult to have a normal relationship with him because he was always slagging off my mum. I feel

quite happy now, and I don't feel I've missed out by not having him around all the time. I've discovered that when I do see him I can talk to him about most things. I even told him when I started my periods and he was really cool about it."
Jane (15)

I always feel upset when I visit Mum

It can be disruptive having "two" homes, especially to start with. If visiting your parent is painful or upsetting then you should discuss the situation with both parents. If this is impossible, ask a third party to intervene. No one should be forced to visit if they don't want to.

Going home again after seeing the absent parent can make you feel sad, but holding on to the fact that you will be seeing them again soon, and making plans, can help.

I want to be with my mates

As you get older, it's natural to want to spend more time with people of your own age. You should be able to organise your visits yourself to take account of what you feel you need, your social life etc rather than being bound by the lifestyle of your parent. Don't feel that doing so makes you disloyal.

Chris found that it was a problem pleasing both his father and himself. He felt really guilty because he was bored when he was with his dad.

"I spend every weekend with my dad. We really get on, and I know he enjoys my visits. The trouble is, I end up feeling really bored. Dad makes me feel guilty because on a Saturday night I want to go out with my mates, not sit at home and watch TV however much he likes having me around."

Chris (15)

However guilty you feel, you must consider yourself too. As a teenager you are beginning to be independent of your parents and form close relationships outside your family. Making the break from a single parent can be particularly difficult. Chris's dad felt lonely and wanted his son's company. Luckily, Chris himself didn't feel under too much pressure and he spoke to his dad, and said that he would be out with his mates on Saturday. His dad was disappointed at first, but he soon got used to it, and on a Sunday Chris was much better company as he felt more cheerful.

eight

*F*acing the world

What Will Friends Think?

"I didn't want to tell anybody at first. I was really embarrassed. But of course, it was dumb, because lots of people at school have divorced parents."
Louise (16)

When the split occurs you will find that you not only have to deal with your emotions and practical changes but also with the attitudes of people outside the immediate family. You may be pleasantly surprised, or terribly disappointed by the reactions of other people. Support for you may come from the oddest quarters. With divorce being so common, people will probably just accept it.

You'll probably get loads of sympathy from your friends to start with, but people's memories are short, and, unless they've experienced it themselves, they don't realise how long it takes to get over it.

Some people can be unnecessarily "cutting" and perhaps even a bit nasty. Remember that they may be reacting through fear – fear that it could happen to them and this is where you have to be more understanding.

"I kept up a front wherever I went. I didn't make it obvious that I was upset inside. I just wanted to be left alone. I didn't tell anyone for a long time. Not even my best friend and she has always been there for me. I just couldn't. I used to sit away from my friends at school, and think about what it would be like if my mum and dad were still together. Once, when my friends asked me what was wrong, I just said nothing and tried to shake it off. Then one day I just came straight out with it."
Louise (16)

It's very natural to feel embarrassed and uncomfortable if one parent leaves. However, it's not your fault and while there is still some stigma attached to divorce, not many people will pass a moral judgement. Most people will understand as it's so common these days. Sometimes friends want to help, but don't know what to say or do.

It's a good idea to tell your friends what's going on, however hard it is. Hiding the truth can get really complicated. Friends can be very supportive, and some may well have been through similar experiences themselves.

"I only told my friends who were really close. My best friend was very understanding. She's been through it herself, and I felt much better telling someone who knew what I was on about."
Jane (15)

"My friends were nice and they didn't make a big deal about it but made sure I was OK. I was never bullied because of it."
Louise (16)

> *"I was really casual. Some friends asked why I was moving and I brought it up then."*
> **Michael (18)**

Telling Other People

> *"Talk to my teacher? No way!"*
> **Paula (15)**

Do your teachers know about the split? Your parents will probably tell your teachers but you might think seriously about talking to them too, particularly if you find that you're working less hard or doing less well than usual. Teachers will be sympathetic if they know what's going on at home. If they don't they may believe that you are simply being lazy.

> *"I felt pretty depressed. I didn't bother with my homework and of course, my grades went down. My tutor asked me what was up. I thought he was going to be really nasty, but I told him my parents had just split up, and we got talking about it. I felt much better after that. He was dead nice."*
> **Tony (16)**

Putting On A Brave Face

> *"After the divorce I moved to a new house and changed schools. I was totally miserable and I didn't tell anyone at first that my parents were divorced. I was dead cool, and if anyone asked me if anything was wrong I said*

no. After I discovered other people in my class had parents who were divorced I felt better."
Paula (15)

"I was worried people would think differently of me if they knew, so I avoided their questions. Then I decided that it was best to be up front – just give straight answers. Nobody mentioned it after that, and I realised it wasn't a big deal."
John (16)

Some teenagers find that the change in their situation can affect their behaviour. They cover up their feelings because they are frightened of what people might think, and what the future holds, but as Paula and John found out, it is so much better to tell everyone.

QUIZ: How Good Are You At Showing Your Emotions?

What kind of person are you? When you come up against a difficult situation how do you react. Do you hit the roof, do you try to be level-headed and reasonable about it, or do you brood quietly, keeping your feelings secret?

1. Your best mate cheats on you with his/her boyfriend/girlfriend. Do you:
   a) tell him/her where to get off?
   b) have a quiet cry about it, then try to put it down to experience?
   c) say nothing, but slip into depression?

---

2. If your cat, dog or friendly pet dies, do you:
    a) have a good cry and hold a funeral service?
    b) dispose of the body and make a decision to get another one as soon as possible?
    c) try to forget the dead?

3. Your boyfriend/girlfriend tells you that his/her ex is constantly calling up just to talk. Do you:
    a) tell your boyfriend/girlfriend that he/she should tell his/her ex to shove off?
    b) tell yourself you're not the jealous type and you trust him/her completely?
    c) say nothing and continue to smile sweetly?

4. You're late meeting a mate and he/she has a go at you. Do you:
    a) storm off in a huff and spend the evening in front of the telly?
    b) tell him/her to calm down and explain why you're late?
    c) say nothing but spend the night feeling guilty?

5. You've had a lot of late nights, you're feeling shattered. A mate calls you and asks you to a party. Do you:
    a) go along but make it clear over and over again that you're doing him/her a big favour?

b) explain that you're having an early night and take a raincheck?

c) you can't say no, so you go along and try to enjoy yourself, hating every minute?

6. You meet someone you really fancy. When you catch his/her eye do you:

a) flirt outrageously and draw as much attention to yourself as you can?

b) smile?

c) look the other way?

7. You've seen these terrific must-have trainers, but your allowance won't cover the cost. Do you:

a) have a major tantrum and demand that your parent gives you the extra money?

b) make up your mind to take that Saturday job and pay for them yourself?

c) go to your room and sulk?

How did you score?
Mostly "a"s. You're obviously the tantrum king/queen, you don't believe in hiding your emotions ever and will always behave as

outrageously as you can. Just remember that going over the top isn't necessarily the way to get what you want.

Mostly "b"s. You're Mr/Ms Cool. You don't indulge in tantrums and you've got the good sense to solve your problems practically.

Mostly "c"s. People find you well-adjusted and easy going. Secretly though, you are a sulk and you are someone who can't let anyone know how you feel. This is dangerous. Denying your feelings is depriving you of many things, not least the ability to enjoy your life.

nine

Old, free and single parents

"Everything changed. We didn't have much money so we moved to a flat and Mum had to work. She never worked when we were small but now she's got her career going again I can see that she's a lot happier because she's a lot more free and individual and able to do her own thing."
Paula (15)

When your parents split up, it's likely that one, or both, will be single for the first time in quite a few years. Some parents settle very happily and normally into their single state, but for others it can take a bit longer. They might behave oddly – and even worse, they might start dating!

Weird Parent Behaviour

It's very common for the newly divorced or separated to act young again, particularly if they've spent months, even years trapped in an unhappy relationship. Imagine the feeling – freedom. Your parent is finally divorced, their money is their own and they can now get on with their life. Why should they wallow in self-pity? They might go a bit over the top. It'll probably make you cringe, but don't worry – it's unlikely to last!

Nevertheless it usually comes as a real surprise when your parent starts dating.

Parents Dating

"Mum seems to go out almost every night. I don't like it. She brings the blokes back sometimes."
Jessica (15)

"How could she get involved with someone so soon after the divorce? I hate him, the boyfriend. He's a creep. I imagine them having sex, it's disgusting. I'm doing everything I can to make him go away."
Carla (14)

Ruining your parent's relationship, like Carla is trying to do, is not a good idea. How would you feel if your parents told you that you couldn't date?

From your point of view it's probably very difficult to think of your parents *ever* dating, so that when they do start again it doesn't seem right.

Often, dating can seem like a betrayal. Things have just happened too fast. That may be true, but if you can, think about it from your parent's point of view.

• Your mum or dad might be really lonely, like Carla's mum.

• They might miss having sex (which you probably can't bear to think about).

• They haven't got used to being single, and want to find a new partner with whom to start a new relationship.

- They feel unconfident and worthless – especially if they were left for someone else. They need to feel attractive.

"I don't think Mum liked herself very much. Dad was always putting her down and she believed it. All those men she went with, I think she was trying to prove she was still attractive or something."
   Olivia (15)

It's very common for the newly single parent to have many partners. However, your parent isn't going to have multiple partners forever. Sooner or later most of them settle down into one special relationship.
   Lizzie's parents split up when she was 14, and she lived with her dad.

"Dad has always been very open about sex, and he made no secret about bringing women home. I didn't like it. I'd come in and find Dad snogging on the sofa. I didn't particularly want him to bring his women home, but I never said anything, I just accepted it. I felt very relieved when he met Caroline. They've been together for three years now, and seem very happy."
   Lizzie (18)

Gay Parents

You might not know one of them is gay until your parents split up and start dating again.
"When Dad told me he was gay, it didn't make me feel any differently about him, I just accepted it. I feel quite happy about it."
   Jamie (15)

Very few gays are awarded custody of children even when there is evidence of good parenting and a close relationship between parent and child. Unfortunately, society still holds a prejudiced and ignorant view of the same-sex family. The truth is that a gay family can be as loving and caring as a heterosexual one.

Jamie's parents separated when he was 13 and his dad moved in with his lover.

"I live with my mum, but I spend weekends with my dad and his partner. I get on really well with both my parents. I don't think there are any differences between ourselves and other families."
Jamie (15)

It is probably wise to take care whom you tell. Don't leave yourself open to teasing or bullying from ignorant people.

"We decided to keep it quiet in case Dad was gay-bashed. My big worry was that I would lose my friends if they knew. I've told my friends. Most are fine, but others try and wind me up. The teachers at school are supportive. My advice to kids who are getting hassled because one of their parents is gay is to ignore it. It doesn't change the way your parents feel about you. They still love you."
Jamie (15)

Parents' New Relationships

"At first, Mum's boyfriends were like clones of my dad. That was OK as far as I'm concerned. It was more

difficult for me when she took up with some guy who was a real div. She still sees him sometimes."
Olivia (15)

The chances are that at some point your parents will have new relationships. Try not to compare them with your other parent, however hard it might be. Don't automatically hate them, even if your dad or mum's new partner was partly responsible for the break-up.

You probably love your parents no matter what they have done, and it's easier all round if you try and get on with their new partner. Ask yourself why you're so against the new relationship. Are you worried that if your parent falls in love he/she will love you less? Are you afraid that they might remarry and have a new family? Once you've acknowledged your fears, then you can deal with them.

And remember, your opinion had no affect on your parents' decision to divorce and your opinion will have little affect on your parents' new relationships. Decide to make the best of it. Remember you have a life to live and it isn't worth you hassling everyone else about decisions which you can't alter.

They might even decide to make their new relationship more permanent...

ten
Step by Step

There are around two and a half million children growing up in step-families in the UK. Step-families can be full time, or part time, perhaps meeting only at weekends or during school holidays, but whatever type they are they can be quite challenging, particularly to start with.

The most important thing to remember is that both you, your parent, your step-parent and step-siblings (if you have any) are going to have very strong but mixed feelings over the change. On the one hand, you might be looking forward to the arrival of a new parent, but on the other you will probably be reluctant to take on the changes that will inevitably follow. Your parent and step-parent will of course be hoping that everything will work out for the best.

How Do You Feel About The Marriage?

"At first I was afraid that my step-dad was going to be a really horrible person, and use my mum and every-thing. I think it's because I'd heard so many awful things about step-families. You know, kids getting sexually abused by their step-parents and everything."
Stephen (16)

It's very common to feel:

- SAD

  While neither of your parents is in a permanent relationship, you can still dream that they'll get back together. You can't any more.

- JEALOUS

  Having gone through the trauma of divorce or separation with your parent, and living with that parent only, you will probably have developed a very close relationship. Not surprisingly, the appearance of a new man or woman can be a shock, and you may feel as if you are being displaced and pushed into second place. Jealousy can range from a slight feeling of discomfort to a full blown sense of bitterness and betrayal.

- ANGRY

  "I couldn't believe that Mum liked Mike more than my dad and I hated him. Whenever he came to the house, I'd give him lip. Mum got really annoyed, but I didn't care."
  Jessica (15)

  You're particularly likely to feel angry if you feel that the step-parent is taking the place of the absent parent.

  "Then Mike moved in. I got really annoyed. He treated the place like it was his own. I felt really angry. I'd been through enough without having to get used to some bloke about the place."
  Jessica (15)

These feelings are all normal. Acknowledge them and talk about them. You might also feel:

* HOPEFUL

  "My dad never had time for us. Like he'd never come to see me in the school play. He always had some excuse, work usually. I really thought my step-dad would be different."

  Rachel (16)

You might hope that the new member of the family will be able to provide you with the things your absent parent wasn't able to give you.

If you hope for too much you may be disappointed. Accept that your step-parent is only human, and can never make up for everything that has happened.

Step-parents

My mum's being replaced

For many teenagers, being part of a step-family is not something they look forward to or enjoy, particularly after a painful event such as a divorce. Janet's dad married again soon after he split up from her mum.

"Sharon wasn't my mum, never could be my mum. I think I hurt her a lot, because she wanted to get close, and I wouldn't let her. I think if she had been my real mum she'd have been pretty good."

Janet (14)

Janet, who lived with her father, refused to have anything to do with her. Whenever Sharon came over she would disappear into her room and stay there. The situation got worse when Sharon moved in.

"I felt I'd already been through a lot of changes, and now I was expected to accept this person living in our house. I didn't want another mum."
   Janet (14)

Janet felt that her mum was being replaced. This was untrue. It's important to remember that just because you have another family, it doesn't mean the old one doesn't exist any more. Your parents will always be your parents. A step-mum or dad doesn't replace your real mum or dad. You don't have to like them or love them, but you should try to respect them and obey the rules.

My step-mother doesn't like me

"I sort of get along with her, but it's hard because she doesn't seem bothered if I'm there or not."
   Kate (12)

Have you got a wicked step-mother? Why do you think the myth of the wicked step-mother is such a powerful one? Remember Hansel and Gretel whose step-mother hated them and plotted to get rid of them? While you might find yourself in a similar situation to Kate the reality is – it's almost certainly not true. Your step-parent is not a monster. It may seem difficult to believe, but in fact he or she wants, if possible, to have a good relationship with you.

   Think about it from their point of view. Step-parenting can be tough – particularly step-parenting when teenagers are involved. It's as new to them as it is to you and they are probably very anxious about how they are going to cope, particularly if they feel you resent them being there and everything they do is wrong. They need all the friends they can get. Getting used to the changes will be difficult at first, but with a little bit of time and effort you might discover that your step-parent's not so bad after all. You might even get to like them.

My step-mum's so strict

There will be lots of changes, and nobody says it's going to be easy. Rules might change from what you've been used to. Gradually, your step-family and you will begin to adopt new rules to suit the new set-up, for example TV watching, staying out late, homework etc. Everyone needs to agree on what these rules are, and what sanctions are applied if they are broken. There will have to be give and take on both sides. Sure, from your point of view your step-parents don't have the same rights as your parents, but as far as your step-parent is concerned, there will sometimes be occasions when they feel that they have to lay down the law. The only way to sort out problems is to talk about them. If you feel for example, that some of the new rules are unfair then discuss them with your parent and step-parent and work out a mutually acceptable solution.

If you feel your natural parent is the only one who can lay down the rules, then you should discuss this rather than have an argument or sulk with the step-parent.

Dad's really changed

"When Dad married Claire, he really changed."
Kate (12)

A step-parent can bring out sides of your parent's personality you've never seen before. Different people do bring out different sides to people – think how you change depending on who you're with. Still, it can be worrying and it takes some getting used to. If you can, spend some time alone with your parent to discuss how they've changed and how it makes you feel.

You might even find they improve in quite a lot of ways.

"My dad was dead untidy. He left his dirty clothes on the floor and his muddy boots in the kitchen. Yuk! My mum always put up with it, but my step-mum – she made him pick his own stuff up and clean his own boots."
Mark (15)

Now I know her better, she's OK

"I hated my step-mum, Sharon, but now I know her better, I think she's really sweet and nice. There are some things we disagree on and she aggravates me a lot, but she's OK really."
Janet (14)

The teenagers who contributed to this book who got along with their step-parent best agreed that they were like a good friend, ie someone who could give them help or advice, provide a shoulder to cry on and perhaps even share hobbies and interests with. As a friend, the step-parent could criticise and give advice, but they didn't assume the authority of a parent.

Step-siblings

Did your step-mum or dad come complete with kids? Accepting a step-brother or sister can be very hard.

My step-sister's boring

"I felt really angry when Mum told us Steph, my step-sister, was coming to live here. I found it hard at first. Steph practically lived in her room and she wouldn't talk to anyone and was really boring."
Donna (14)

It took some time and effort but eventually Donna discovered that because both of them had been through a hard time when their parents divorced, they actually had something in common and they became good friends. Not that there aren't problems to be overcome. When her mum re-married, Donna had to share a room with her step-sister. She didn't like it, but tried hard to accept it.

She spoils my step-sister

"My step-sister's always using my make-up or borrowing my clothes and it really makes me angry. I told my mum, but she didn't think it was a big deal. I wish she wouldn't always take my step-sister's side."
Donna (14)

You might find that your mum or dad bends over backwards to try and be fair to their step-child and not show favouritism to you. This might make them unintentionally go the other way and give you a harder time. Donna's case is typical. Donna felt that her mum had taken her step-sister's side against her because she seemed so uninterested in how she felt and therefore her mum obviously cared more about her step-sister than her. In fact Donna's mum was so anxious to get along with her step-daughter that she tended to be hard on her own child. Once she realised that Donna wasn't being mean but felt genuinely aggrieved, she was able to talk to her step-daughter and tell her to ask Donna first before she borrowed anything.

"When I visited Dad, it was fun having a step-brother to do things with, but my father wasn't there for me. He showed favouritism to my step-brother. He spent more time with him than me. I really felt pushed into the background."
Jason (16)

"The bad things were the jealousy and favouritism. I think my step-brother had a good deal. As he was the new one of the family they (the parents) made a big fuss of him."
Mark (15)

"I was an only child before, but my step-father has two kids of his own. At first it was weird but now I like being a member of a big family, even if one of them is a complete dork."
Tina (15)

...And A Baby

It brought me and my step-brothers together

"I was gob-smacked when Mum told us she was pregnant. So were my step-brothers. None of us liked it. It was the first time we had agreed on anything.We were pretty mean to Mum during her pregnancy."
Rachel (16)

As Rachel and her step-brothers saw it, her mother and step-father were creating a third family to which none of them felt they belonged. They felt pushed out, and bound up together in mutual hate of the situation. They worried that their parents wouldn't love them as much as the new baby.

"Amazingly, when Pete was born, it brought us together because we felt he belonged to both families."
Rachel (16)

"I think it's nice. I enjoy being second eldest and I consider my half-brothers and sisters as my real brothers and sisters and would never treat them below my real brother because they are just as important to me. Best of all is that my half-brothers and sisters and my step-mum can give me relief and a different type of relationship than I get with my real family."
Louise (16)

Sexuality In The Step-family

"My father and my step-mother would kiss on the sofa - yuk!"
Jade (18)

Sexuality is important in all families, but in step-families it can require some attention. This is not because the issue of sex is wildly different from other families, rather because it sometimes becomes more obvious.

Everyone feels at some time, how weird it is that their parents have sex. Some teenagers think it's pretty disgusting. If your parent has remarried you might find it very difficult to accept that he/she is sexually active. You might want to leave the room if they touch each other. You may experience twinges of jealousy – sex and jealousy are obviously linked together in this situation, particularly if feelings of jealousy already exist.

This combination of your own sexual feeling and that of your parent and step-parent can be pretty explosive. Sex is difficult to talk about in most families, but more so in step-families. Mothers and daughters seem far more relaxed and more likely to be able to talk about sex than sons and fathers. If you can't talk openly to your parents, talk to a friend or call an advice line. (See Chapter 12)

My step-dad would come into the bathroom

"I felt really embarrassed. My step-dad would walk round the house with nothing on or come into the bathroom when he knew I was there."
Natasha (15)

Another dimension on sex has to do with possible feelings of sexual attraction between adults and teenagers. In unbroken families parents have seen their children grow up from babyhood, and such feelings are very unlikely to exist. This is more difficult in the step-family, where the adult only knows the teenager. Your step-parent should not express any interest in you sexually, but if you find yourself in that position, don't keep it to yourself, talk to someone – your natural parent if possible, or a friend or teacher. Most teenagers will find this a difficult thing to do, but it must be dealt with.

The question of sexual abuse can't be ignored. Most of us believe that such a thing could never happen in our family, but there is clear evidence that it goes on a lot more than we think. One example can occur when a stepfather uses his sexuality as a weapon either to seduce his step-daughter or as a way of getting his step-daughter on his side in family arguments. A sexual relationship between a step-parent and teenager is wrong in every way. The only way to get away from abuse is to tell someone. You must protect yourself.

I fancy my step-brother

"My step-brother was absolutely gorgeous. Not like his dad who's a complete nerd."
Jade (18)

It's quite common for teenagers in step-families to find themselves attracted to one another. Although they're not illegal, these relationships are very difficult. It's best to avoid them if you can. At your age, you're probably not looking for a permanent relationship, you're still experimenting. Remember that when the relationship ends, you're still going to be step-siblings.

The Top Ten Tips For Surviving Your Step-family

1   Be tolerant.

2   Remember that no one expects you to love your step-family.

3   Be kind.

4   Try and obey the rules.

5   Remember that it's just as tough for them as it is for you.

6   Be honest about how you feel. Don't bottle up angry or resentful feelings. If something bothers you, talk about it and try to work it out.

7   Don't be too hard on yourself. Remember that it's going to take time to get used to the changes.

8   At some time, it's usual for families to reach crisis point. Try to remember that this is temporary and things will settle down.

9   If you have to share a room with a step-sibling, try and reach a compromise.

10. Have a sense of humour.

---

eleven

I Will Survive

While you are going through a family break-up it often feels as if your whole world is shattered. You feel your life is a total mess, and things will never be the same again. Everyone's emotions are in chaos, nobody knows what to do. How do you cope?

Well, you do. Most people are survivors and tough experiences are part of life. As we deal with them we grow as people and learn to cope better with whatever hand life deals us. Frequently people find that they've gained something positive from the experience.

Many young people think their experiences have made them more mature and independent earlier, and that this has enabled them to become wiser and more able to cope with life's problems.

It's Not All Bad!

"My sister and I never really talked much. She's a couple of years younger than me and I thought she was a real baby. When Mum and Dad split up, she was the only person who understood me and we really got to know each other. She's my best friend now."

Jade (18)

"I actually enjoy seeing my parents separately. I spend more time with them now, and they make a real effort

to do things like taking me to places that I like."
Louise (16)

"I've become far more grown up in a lot of ways because I've had to solve a lot of problems which might not have happened if they hadn't divorced. "
Janet (15)

"In many ways I see my mum as a person who I really like, and talk to. Before she was just there."
John (16)

"I was an only child before – and it's great having some step-brothers around."
Tina (15)

"I have changed. I had to be strong and supportive when they started leaning on me – sharing their problems with me – and it made me grow up a lot."
Jane (15)

"I'm a lot stronger and less naive. I had to be more independent, and I was shown the world as it really is."
Rachel (16)

Helping Yourself

Keep talking

"Talk to someone. It always helps to have someone to lean on."
Lizzie (18)

Talking is probably the most positive way you can help yourself. Talking about a problem nearly always makes you feel better. Hiding it makes you feel worse.

Acknowledging your fears, thinking and talking about them, however difficult and distressing it may be, helps you feel more in control of your life. Feelings left unexplored, slowly but surely fester inside and could seriously damage your relationships with those around you. You have to remember, too, that talking about these feelings once or twice won't be enough; "talk" will be most helpful and effective if you can do it on as many different occasions as possible, and under as many different circumstances as you can find. The painful feelings that often result from divorce need much courage, time and patience to work through.

Write it down

Everyone's life story is happy and sad, and you can't pretend the bad things didn't happen. Some people never talk about the past, and everyone's memory can play tricks, but if you have something written down, it will help now and in the future.

Your autobiography might possibly take the following form:

- A DIARY with entries made as often as you like, charting what's going on, how you are feeling and the changes you are experiencing.

- MY LIFE STORY. This is an album or scrapbook of your life.

Here are a few things you might include:

- A family tree. Include your half-siblings, if you have them, even your step-family.

- Family photos, pictures, letters and other memorabilia to remind you what your parents used to look like, and favourite places you visited together.

- Anecdotes and stories of funny or special things that have happened.

Other People Who Can Help

There are a lot of people around you could talk to who can sympathise, and give you advice if you want it.

- Your parents

  Often when you have problems parents are the most obvious people to turn to. But divorce concerns them, and is a hard time for them. Bear in mind that they might find talking difficult. At the time of the break-up many parents are not able to give their children sufficient attention.

- Family or friends

  Sisters or brothers can be a real support – they will understand what you feel because they are going through exactly the same experience. What about your best friend? Other people of your own age who have gone through a similar experience are great – knowing that you're not the only one to find themselves in this situation makes you feel less isolated. It also helps to learn that people do recover.

- Professionals

  Sometimes the advice you get from somebody who doesn't know you or your family intimately can be more valuable than either friends or relatives. These people could include a teacher at school, a doctor or a counsellor. There are also organisations you can contact, such as those listed in the back of this book.

Don't be afraid to ask for help. People usually like to be asked, although they don't always offer help in case you don't want it.

"After seeing a counsellor, I can now cope with other issues and talk to people more easily."
Jessica (15)

Don't let anyone accuse you of being selfish. This is a time to really examine what you want and what you think you need.

"For once in your life think about yourself and no one else. Talk to as many people as you can and hold on because if you do it'll be over before you know it."
Lizzie (18)

"You have to work out what's best for yourself, tell your parents and don't let them mess you up."
Freddie (14)

Teenage Advice

In the questionnaire I prepared to gather information for this book, I specifically asked teenagers what help or advice they would give a friend who was experiencing the crisis of their parents' separation or divorce. Here's a selection of the answers:

"Just try and be positive about it."
Paula (15)

"Talk about it. Don't bottle up your feelings. It's important to be honest about how you feel."
Tess (20)

"Don't be embarrassed about having divorced parents. It's sad, but it's not the end of the world."
   Jessica (15)

"Don't worry about it, it's not your fault and things will get better soon."
   Louise (16)

"Sympathise with your parents, and let them do what is best for them and for you."
   Jamie (15)

Looking To The Future

Don't feel embarrassed. A lot of young people feel that having divorced parents is a stigma. One in three couples get divorced so a lot of people don't have two parents living together.

Tess's parents divorced when she was thirteen. Now twenty, she is able to look back and put things in perspective.

"If people can't live in harmony and do not see eye to eye, it's best for all concerned for the parents to go their separate ways. It doesn't seem like it at the time, but looking back it is."
   Tess (20)

Many teenagers also worry that having seen their parents separate, their own relationships will be doomed to failure. Although there is some evidence to show that the children of divorcees are more likely to go through a divorce themselves, it doesn't necessarily mean it's going to happen to you. Don't forget that most important of all is the type of person you are, what kind of family you come from, and the way you relate to one another.

Although it is useful to observe a good relationship in action the reverse is true too. If you watch your parents make the same mistakes over and over again, you learn what not to do!

The Top Ten Survival Guide

1 Other people have come through a family break-up and survived – so will you.

2 Life isn't perfect. Try to accept that life has its ups and downs.

3 Bad things will happen but the good things will help you get over them.

4 Keep saying to yourself, "This too, will pass". Time has a way of making things better.

5 Don't go on a guilt trip. It's not your fault.

6 Make sure you get as much information as possible, so that you know what's going on.

7 Make decisions that are right for you.

8 Don't expect perfection. Real life isn't like a Hollywood movie. Families, including step-families, aren't always sweetness and light.

9 Accept that change takes time.

10 Once everything is worked out, you can go on living.

A Last Word...

In time, you and your parents will grow to accept the changes. The new school, home, step-family may even become as familiar as the old one.

Often, separation or divorce is for the best, so try to focus on the fact that once you've come through it, and recover, you might even find life is better than it was before.

Let Louise have the last word:

"Even though things have been bad, I don't think I've ever regretted my parents getting divorced. They never could get along. The rows were awful. It's better without all that. Sure, I wish they could have been more friendly, but things turned out different. The best thing to come out of it is that Mum and I are much closer than we used to be. We get on really well. Getting divorced is not the end of the world, it hasn't put me off marriage, but I hope I never have to go through it myself."
   Louise (16)

twelve

*H*elp

The Law In England, Wales And Northern Ireland

The time it takes for a divorce to become final takes between five months and two years. If your parents simply separate, there are no legal formalities, and they are free to make their own arrangements.

However, for a divorce to be granted the law has to be satisfied that the marriage has "irretrievably broken down" to such an extent that it cannot be mended and that satisfactory financial arrangements and arrangements for children have been made.

The law states that one or more of the following reasons for divorce must apply:

1. Adultery – that is when sexual intercourse has occurred between a married partner and someone who is not their partner.

2. Either party has behaved "unreasonably" – for example if one partner has behaved violently, gambled away money or has a drink or drug problem.

3. One partner has deserted the other for two years or more.

4. A couple has lived apart for at least two years and both agree to a divorce – this is known as a "no fault divorce".

5. The couple has lived apart for five years, and one does not agree to a divorce.

What rights do teenagers have?

When considering whether to grant a divorce petition, the Court will look at all the circumstances, but the most important aspect will be the welfare of any children in the family under the age of majority – 18 years old. That means YOU!

Prior to 1989, the Court simply made "orders" regulating where the children were to live, and what contact each parent would have with them. However, the Children Act which came into force in 1989, changed all that.

The primary aim of the Children Act has been to take the responsibility of deciding what is to be done with the children away from the Court, and place it squarely on the shoulders of the parents.

If you were born within your parents' marriage, both of them will have certain rights and obligations towards you. Between them, they must sort out where your home is going to be, and how you will be provided for financially. One parent usually cares for you on a day-to-day basis, and sees that you are provided with everything you need (food, shelter etc) while the other usually contributes towards the cost. Whichever parent you live with, the other will still have the right to participate in major decision making – such as the sort of education you are going to have – and arrangements will be made for you to see them on a regular basis.

However, if your parents cannot agree and problems arise, the case will go before the Court, and a judge will decide on what he or she feels is in your best interests. A Welfare Report will be compiled, and you will certainly be asked for your views and your preferences.

Making a choice

It's easiest if your parents decide between themselves who you live with. But maybe they can't agree, or they ask you where you want to live. This can be very difficult as you feel disloyal to one if you choose the other. You have to decide where you would feel happiest and most secure.

As a teenager, your views will certainly be the prime consideration of the Court. As a general rule, if you express a preference the Court will concede to your wishes, unless there are very good reasons to do otherwise – in cases of abuse for example. Therefore, if you have strong feelings or good reasons for your preferences, it's very important to speak up.

The first appointment at Court will generally be a "conciliation appointment". You will be expected to attend with your parents to discuss your views. You will also have a private, confidential meeting, without your parents, where you can put forward your views on who you want to live with etc. Although this may be frightening, remember that the conciliation officer is there to help you. He/she works with teenagers like you a great deal, and will certainly be aware of how you feel.

The Court rarely splits up siblings, so it's unlikely you will be separated from your sisters or brothers.

Once a "residence order" (saying which parent you are to live with) has been awarded, the Court will grant a "contact order" which will give the non-custodial parent the right to see you. Occasionally the Court decides that it would be dangerous for you to have contact with the other parent – for example if there has been a history of abuse.

The Law In Scotland

While the grounds for divorce, and some aspects of the proceedings are much the same as those in England and Wales, there are some important differences between English and Scottish law.

The Children Act does not apply in Scotland and parents are considered joint guardians with joint custody of the children. In order for a divorce to be granted, the Court must be satisfied that both your parents have made suitable arrangements for you – where you are going to live, who is going to look after you and how. In addition, they require a sworn statement, known as an "affidavit" from a neighbour or someone who knows you well. If the affidavit is accepted, neither you nor your parents will be interviewed. The Court will only interfere if any of these arrangements break down. Once you reach the age of 16 you can live where you like, handle your own money and make your own decisions.

Useful Addresses

These agencies can give you confidential advice and support. They are run by understanding, experienced people who genuinely want to help you.

0800 numbers can be dialled free of charge (you don't need a phonecard or money) and won't show up on the phone bill; other numbers are charged at the normal rate. If you live outside London, it's still worth dialling a London number. You can call London numbers to obtain information because many of these organisations have local branches, and will give you a local number to call. Remember that sometimes these numbers are very busy, so if you can't get through at first, keep trying.

Alateen

61 Great Dover Street
London SE1 4YF
0171 403 0888

24-hour confidential helpline for the family and friends of alcoholics.

Brook Advisory Centres

for contraceptive advice, counselling and referral to local branches.

0171 713 9000
Mon-Fri 9-5pm

Childline

24-hour free helpline.
Freephone 0800 1111

Children's Legal Centre

for information on custody, the law and your legal rights.

University of Essex
Wivenhoe Park
Colchester
Essex CO4 3SQ
01206 873 820

Advice line open Mon-Fri 2-5pm, Mon, Wed, Fri 10am-12 noon and Tue and Thurs 5-7pm.

Gingerbread

A national self-help organisation for one parent families.

16-17 Clerkenwell Close
London EC1R 0AA

0171 336 8183

Advice line open Mon, Tue 11am-4pm, Wed 10am-12 noon, Thurs 10am-4pm

Lesbian and Gay Switchboard

0171 837 7324

National Step-family Association

for counselling and referral to local branches

Chapel House
18 Hatton Place
London EC1 8RU

0171 209 2460

Counselling helpline 0171 209 2464

open Mon-Fri 2pm-5pm & 7pm-10pm

Scottish Council For Single Parents

Advice, information & referral
13 Gayfield Square
Edinburgh EH1 3NX

0131 556 3899

Further Reading

Dealing with Family Break Up by Kate Haycock (Wayland, 1995)

Divorce and Your Children by Anne Hooper (Robson Books, 1981)

It's Not Your Fault by Rosemary Stones (Piccadilly Press, 1994)

When Parents Split Up: Divorce Explained to Young People by Ann Mitchell (Chambers 1986)

The Which? Guide to Divorce by Helen Garlick (Consumer's Association, 1996)

The Seven Stages of Divorce by Simone E
    Katzenberg, (Solomon, Taylor & Shaw, 1996)
    & *The Seven Stages of Divorce Part 2 - The
    Children* by Simone E Katzenberg, Solomon
    Taylor & Shaw, 1996

Both titles are available from
    3 Coach House Yard
    Hampstead High Street
    London NW3 1QD

Other Materials

Teenagers and Divorce by Dr John Coleman
    (Tapewise (Audio Publications) Ltd), 1996

Teenagers and Step Parents by Dr John Coleman,
    (Tapewise (Audio Publications) Ltd, 1996

Booklet and cassette set available from

    The Trust for the Study of Adolescence
    23 New Rd
    Brighton
    E Sussex BN1 1WZ

Index

Other teenage books

published by

Piccadilly Press

Non-fiction

Speak For Yourself: Finding Your Voice Among Your Peers
by Rosie Rushton

Wouldn't it be wonderful to talk sensibly to the boy of
your dreams? Think great (but true) things about
yourself, rather than thinking what a dork you are? Do
what you want to do, not what everyone else wants you
to do? Well you can!

With confidence you can do anything! Here's how to
get it.

Looking Good: The Ultimate Teenage Beauty Guide
by Vickie Bramwell

*"...a fab book about how you can look good without
needing loads of money or make-up!"* – Shout
magazine

Feeling Great: The Teenager's Guide To Glowing Good Health
by Vickie Bramwell

Eating properly, exercising, zit-zapping, staying sweet smelling, common health problems, talking to the doctor...all the information you'll need to know is here.

"...an invaluable handbook...Vickie Bramwell knows her teenage readers well" – The Bookseller

Get Better Grades
by Margie Agnew, Steve Barlow, Lee Pascal and Steve Skidmore

"Teenager friendly and witty, the book teems with quizzes, mock agony aunts, cartoons and amusing advice on how to remember things..." – Independent

Action Replays
by Steve Barlow, Iain Carter and Steve Skidmore

Find out the football stars' most significant sporting moments. There are also jokes, blunders and statistics.

Selected by the Bookseller for its Books for Chistmas

Fiction

Just Don't Make A Scene, Mum
by Rosie Rushton

This is the first title in the tremendously popular Leehampton trilogy about five teenagers and their mortifyingly-embarrassing parents.

"...*cool and diverting comedy*" – The Times

I Think I'll Just Curl Up And Die
by Rosie Rushton

They thought their parents couldn't get any more embarrassing – then they get worse!

"...*she juggles the humour, heartache and heavy-breathing with an easy balance of wit and sympathy*" – Joanna Carey of the Guardian

How Could You Do This To Me, Mum?
by Rosie Rushton

"...*worth every penny for the sheer awful fun of adolescence...I could carry on and on – it's wonderful*" – Books for Keeps

Great! You've Just Ruined The Rest Of My Life
by Yvonne Coppard

"*There is plenty of humour but also wisdom...lively book...will be greatly enjoyed by girls*" – School Librarian

True Romance: A Story Of Love From Both Sides
    by Marina Gask

    Emily and Nathan are crazy about each other, which
    everybody knows except them.

    *"...you'll be cringing with recognition at Emily...there
    are invaluable lessons to be learned – this book could
    seriously improve your love life"* – Guardian

Just published:

Getting A Life
    by Samantha Rugen

    When even your grandmother tells you to get a life, it's
    time to do something about it! Jayne yearns to be a
    proper teenager, but it's not easy. In letters and her
    diary, she shows the joys and pains of being a teenager.

Poppy
    by Rosie Rushton

    Poppy seems to have it all – she's pretty, popular, has a
    model family, and boys queuing up to take her out.

    But how will she cope when her secure environment
    crumbles around her?

    Rosie Rushton writes with tremendous verve and
    empathy about some very nineties problems.

Spin The Bottle

by James Pope

Zoë is in trouble for skipping school, fighting, smoking, messing around in class...

Sally Ward, her form teacher, tries to deal with Zoë's outrageous sense of humour and help her through the year. Sally suggests using their computers as a two-way journal, a means of exchanging thoughts over the problems Zoë has.

But Zoë's problems are far deeper than Sally could have imagined.